$9.99 USD

Dedication

For further information, write to MAC THE RAVEN ENTERPRISES, LLC

P.O. Box 1186

Hoodsport, WA

lindalsund@gmail.com

www.mactheraven.com

Library of Congress Control Number

International Standard Book Number: 978-0-9893597-5-7

Mac Learns To Fly

Our Pet Raven - A True Story

Written By Linda Sund

Illustrated by Denis Proulx

Book 2 of a Series
Sharing stories of Mac's Adventures

Coming soon: "Mac and Clinger", "Mac Meets Fern", "Mac Meets Leanne",
"Mac's First Day At School", "Mac Hikes Mt Ellinor" and more

With much thanks to Misako Yoke
For all your illustration ideas, inspiration, expertise, and your true love for Mac and his stories

Especially for: Rylee, Kale, Sarah, and Trevor
Love, Nana & Papa

Order online   www.mactheraven.com

This is Mac.

He is our pet raven.

Today he is 3 months old

and will learn to fly,

really high, up in the sky.

Mac waits,
sitting on the deck railing,
not making a sound.
He is watching the cat, Clinger,
on the grass,
running and chasing butterflies
all around.

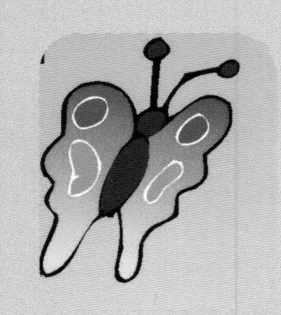

It's breakfast time and Mac
is waiting for his meal.

He is in a good mood

when he sees all that food.

Mac cries with glee

AWK! AWK! AWK!

This morning it is chicken and rice,

what a nice surprise.

Hippity hop, Hippity hop,

Mac gobbles it all up!!

Mama Linda reaches her arm out
for Mac to climb on.

"It's now time for you to learn

to flap your wings and fly,

way up into the sky!"

Mac stretches the left wing

and then the right.

He imagines what it would feel like

to be in flight.

It would be such an incredible sight!!

Mac starts to flap his wings,
slow at first,

and then faster and FASTER.

Linda moves her arm up and down

until Mac lifts off.

He hovers for a moment

but soon falls to the ground.

Mac screeches

AWK! AWK! AWK!

That hurt just a little.

"Try it again! Try it again!"
she says,

as Mac stands on her hand

so he can do it again.

Mac flaps and flaps his wings so hard

that he flies 10 feet in the air,

which is mighty fine.

As Mac comes down from the sky this time,

he lands on Linda's head.

Is this a sign???

Will Mac ever learn how to fly?

Will he someday fly high?

Up, up, up...in the sky???

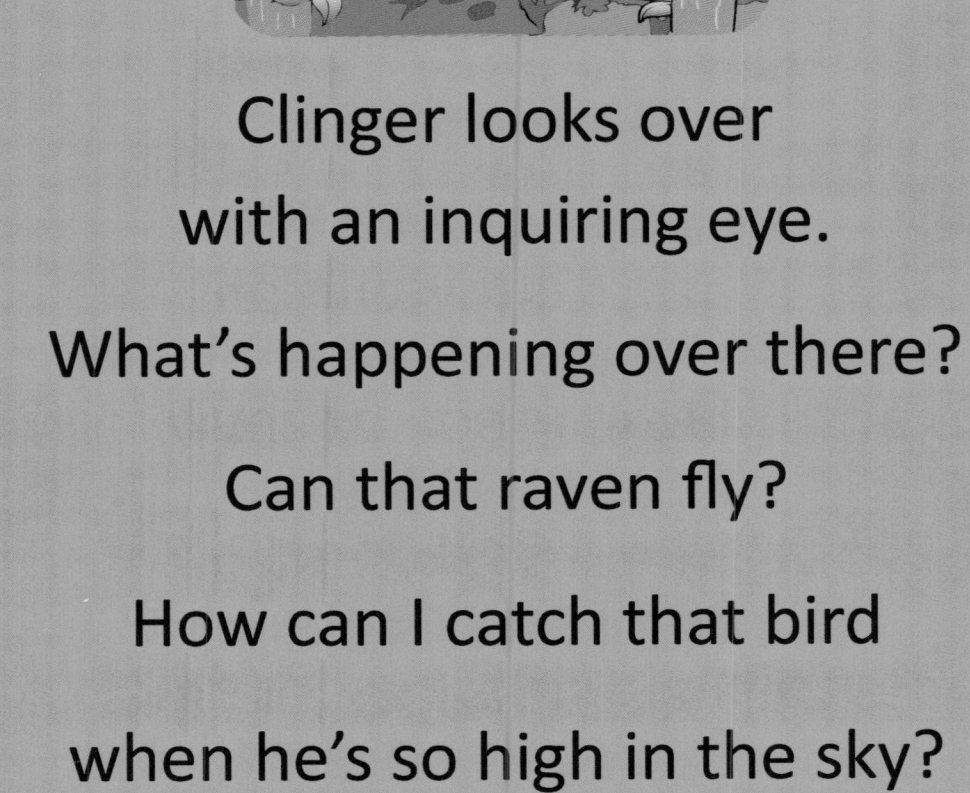

Clinger looks over
with an inquiring eye.

What's happening over there?

Can that raven fly?

How can I catch that bird

when he's so high in the sky?

I can do it! I can do it!

Let's give it one more try!

Linda takes him in her hands

and tosses Mac

way up in the air!!

And there he goes,

high, high, high... He can fly!!

Mac flies above the yard twice,

above the cornfield,

and right over the roof.

He's way up in the sky,

all by himself.

Mac loves to soar through the air

with the breeze in his face

and the wind in his wings.

What a great feeling!

Up, up, he goes, where he will stop,

nobody knows.

Mac sees Mama Linda and Clinger,

who look small on the ground.

He also sees a coin which is shiny and round.

Ruby, the dog, has a worried look on her face.

She wants Mac safe and sound,

and back in his place.

It's now time for Mac
to land in a tree.

Wheeeee, he says,

"LOOK AT ME!"

It's been a big day.
Mac flew down from the tree

to land on Linda's arm,

who was proud as can be.

There will be more fun to come,

in the month of May.

So, please, Mr. Mac,

don't you fly away...

Mac was born in northwest Washington State near Hoodsport.

As a baby, he accidentally fell out of a tree.   Mac was rescued and raised by Brian and Linda Sund, who considered him a part of the family.   Mac loved all the pets in the family.   Ruby the dog, Clinger the cat and a small deer, named Fern. They were all friends.
Fern, as a fawn, was also rescued by the Sunds.
She was saved after being hit by a car near Olympia, WA.

We hope you all enjoy Mac's stories and the adventures of Mac.

Mac is truly a loving, funny and mischievous bird.

He had a big heart and enjoyed all who came to visit.

The End

CPSIA information can be obtained
at www.ICGtesting.com
Printed in the USA
BVIC01210708071B
32317BV00001B

ISBN 978-0-9893597-5-7

9000